Julia Reed

The Global Financial Crisis of 2008

Causes, Consequences, and Lessons for the Modern Economy

ELIVA PRESS

ISBN: 978-99993-4-472-2

Cover Design: Eliva Press
Cover Image: www.ingimage.com
Email: info@elivapress.com
Website: www.elivapress.com

This Eliva Press imprint is published by the registered company Eliva Press Global Ltd. part of Eliva Press S.R.L. Publishing Group

The registered company address is: Pope Hennessy Street Level 2, Hennessy Tower Port Louis, Mauritius
Eliva Press S.R.L. Publishing Group legal address is: Bd. Cuza-Voda 1/4 of. 21, Chisinau, Moldova, Europe

The Global Financial Crisis of 2008

Causes, Consequences, and Lessons for the Modern Economy

The Global Financial Crisis of 2008

Causes, Consequences, and Lessons for the Modern Economy

A concise book-format study

Prepared as an educational overview for students, researchers, and readers interested in financial crises, macroeconomic policy, and institutional reform.

Use Note

This book is an original educational synthesis on the global financial crisis of 2007-2009, commonly known as the 2008 economic crisis. It is written for general academic use and is not financial, legal, or investment advice.

The discussion combines macroeconomic history, banking theory, policy analysis, and institutional lessons. The references section lists major works and official reports that informed the interpretation, including central bank documents, international organization studies, and scholarly books on financial instability.

The goal is not to assign a single cause to a complex event. Rather, the book explains how household borrowing, securitization, leverage, weak supervision, short-term funding, mispriced risk, and global imbalances interacted to create a systemic crisis.

Contents

Preface

The 2008 economic crisis was not merely a stock-market collapse or a temporary failure of mortgage lending. It was a breakdown in the architecture of modern finance. The crisis exposed how private incentives, public regulation, monetary conditions, and global capital flows can reinforce each other in ways that make a system appear stable precisely when it is becoming fragile.

For many readers, the crisis is remembered through visible events: the failure of Lehman Brothers, emergency meetings at central banks, collapsing housing prices, bank rescues, and rising unemployment. Those events were dramatic, but they were the surface expression of deeper institutional weaknesses. A major purpose of this book is to connect the visible events to the underlying mechanisms.

The crisis also changed the language of economic policy. Terms such as liquidity facility, stress test, macroprudential regulation, too big to fail, quantitative easing, moral hazard, systemic risk, and shadow banking became part of public debate. Understanding these terms is essential because they describe not only what happened in 2008 but also how authorities try to prevent the next crisis.

The book proceeds from context to mechanism, from mechanism to policy response, and from policy response to lessons. It explains why the crisis began in the United States housing and mortgage markets, how it spread through global financial networks, why it became an employment and output crisis, and why recovery was uneven across regions and social groups.

A recurring theme is that financial crises are rarely caused by a single mistake. They are more often produced by an accumulation of small permissions: permission to borrow more, to check less, to assume liquidity, to rely on ratings, to believe that housing prices cannot fall nationally, and to trust that private risk models know more than history. When these permissions become embedded in institutions, they can produce systemic failure.

The 2008 crisis therefore remains a vital case study. It is a warning about complacency, a lesson in interdependence, and a reminder that markets are institutional systems requiring rules, transparency, capital, and credible oversight.

Chapter 1 - The World Before the Crisis

The Great Moderation and the Illusion of Stability

The decades before 2008 were often described as a period of the Great Moderation. Inflation appeared lower and more stable, recessions in advanced economies seemed milder, and central banks were widely believed to have learned how to manage the business cycle. This atmosphere encouraged confidence in financial innovation and in the ability of markets to distribute risk efficiently.

However, macroeconomic stability at the surface did not eliminate financial instability below the surface. Low measured volatility reduced the perceived probability of loss. Investors became more willing to accept thin risk premiums, banks expanded balance sheets, and households took on mortgage obligations that depended on continued growth in income or house prices.

One of the central paradoxes of the pre-crisis period is that stability helped generate fragility. When recent history looks safe, lenders and borrowers often extrapolate safety into the future. That is why periods of calm can be fertile ground for leverage, maturity mismatch, and the underpricing of risk.

This point matters because financial crises are cumulative. A single weakness may be manageable, but a set of mutually reinforcing weaknesses can overwhelm ordinary safeguards. For that reason, the 2008 crisis is best understood as a chain of incentives and institutional gaps rather than as a single accident.

Global Imbalances and the Search for Yield

Global capital flows also shaped the environment. Surplus countries accumulated reserves and invested heavily in safe dollar-denominated assets, while deficit countries absorbed capital through financial markets. The demand for apparently safe assets encouraged the production of securities backed by mortgages and other loans.

This search for yield was not limited to aggressive hedge funds. Pension funds, insurance companies, banks, and money market institutions all sought instruments that offered a little more return without appearing to add much risk. Structured finance seemed to meet that desire by transforming pools of loans into securities with different risk levels.

The problem was that the safety of highly rated securities depended on assumptions about correlation, housing prices, refinancing behavior, and market liquidity. When those assumptions failed together, securities that appeared diversified became channels of concentrated systemic risk.

This point matters because financial crises are cumulative. A single weakness may be manageable, but a set of mutually reinforcing weaknesses can overwhelm ordinary safeguards. For that reason, the 2008 crisis is best understood as a chain of incentives and institutional gaps rather than as a single accident.

Housing as a Financial Engine

In the United States, rising housing prices became a financial engine. Homeowners borrowed against appreciated home values, lenders expanded mortgage products, and investors bought securities based on mortgage cash flows. Housing shifted from being primarily a consumption asset to being treated by many households as a source of wealth, collateral, and financial security.

The expansion of housing credit was not uniform. It included traditional mortgages, subprime loans, adjustable-rate mortgages, low-documentation loans, and products that postponed full repayment burdens into the future. The model depended heavily on refinancing and on the assumption that a borrower in trouble could sell or refinance before defaulting.

Once housing prices stopped rising, the logic reversed. Borrowers lost refinancing options, mortgage defaults increased, securities lost value, and financial institutions faced losses on assets that had previously been treated as safe or highly liquid.

This point matters because financial crises are cumulative. A single weakness may be manageable, but a set of mutually reinforcing weaknesses can overwhelm ordinary safeguards. For that reason, the 2008 crisis is best understood as a chain of incentives and institutional gaps rather than as a single accident.

Chapter 2 - Mortgage Markets and Securitization

From Local Lending to Global Securities

Traditional banking often involved a lender that originated a loan and kept it on its balance sheet. In the originate-to-distribute model, the lender could originate a mortgage, sell it into a pool, and allow the cash flows to be packaged into securities purchased by investors around the world. This model increased credit supply but weakened incentives to monitor borrower quality.

Securitization was not inherently harmful. Properly designed, it can diversify funding sources and spread risk. The difficulty before 2008 was that the chain between borrower and final investor became long, complex, and opaque. Each participant could earn fees while passing risk onward.

Complexity made accountability difficult. Mortgage brokers, originators, arrangers, rating agencies, insurers, investment banks, and investors each held a partial view. The system worked as long as defaults remained low and refinancing remained easy. Once defaults rose, the chain transmitted losses rapidly.

This point matters because financial crises are cumulative. A single weakness may be manageable, but a set of mutually reinforcing weaknesses can overwhelm ordinary safeguards. For that reason, the 2008 crisis is best understood as a chain of incentives and institutional gaps rather than as a single accident.

Subprime Lending and Underwriting Weakness

Subprime lending served borrowers with weaker credit histories or limited documentation. Some borrowers could manage such loans, but many products were structured with low introductory payments that later reset to higher rates. These terms made the loan affordable only under optimistic assumptions.

Weak underwriting was a major vulnerability. Loan-to-value ratios rose, income documentation weakened, and lending standards declined in competitive markets. In some cases, lenders relied on the collateral value of the house rather than on the sustainable repayment capacity of the borrower.

This was dangerous because collateral values were themselves driven by the credit boom. Rising prices justified more lending, more lending supported rising prices, and the feedback loop masked the deterioration of loan quality.

This point matters because financial crises are cumulative. A single weakness may be manageable, but a set of mutually reinforcing weaknesses can overwhelm ordinary safeguards. For that reason, the 2008 crisis is best understood as a chain of incentives and institutional gaps rather than as a single accident.

Ratings and Structured Finance

Credit ratings played a central role in the expansion of mortgage-backed securities and collateralized debt obligations. Ratings allowed investors to treat certain securities as low risk, even when the underlying collateral involved risky mortgages. Regulatory frameworks and institutional mandates often depended on ratings.

The models used to rate structured products often underestimated the probability that many mortgages would default together. If housing prices declined nationally, diversification across regions would provide less protection than assumed. The crisis revealed how model risk can become systemic when many institutions rely on similar assumptions.

Rating agencies also faced conflicts of interest because issuers paid for ratings. Although ratings were not the only cause of the crisis, their credibility helped transform risky mortgage exposure into widely held financial assets.

This point matters because financial crises are cumulative. A single weakness may be manageable, but a set of mutually reinforcing weaknesses can overwhelm ordinary safeguards. For that reason, the 2008 crisis is best understood as a chain of incentives and institutional gaps rather than as a single accident.

Chapter 3 - Shadow Banking and Systemic Fragility

What Shadow Banking Means

Shadow banking refers to credit intermediation outside the traditional deposit-funded banking system. It includes investment banks, structured investment vehicles, money market funds, repo markets, securities lenders, and other institutions that perform bank-like functions without the same regulatory structure.

The term does not mean illegal banking. Rather, it describes a system that creates credit and liquidity through market-based mechanisms. Before 2008, shadow banking grew rapidly because it could provide funding efficiently and because many participants believed collateralized short-term markets were safe.

The weakness was that shadow banking depended on confidence. Unlike insured deposits, many forms of shadow funding could disappear quickly. When lenders became uncertain about collateral values or counterparty solvency, funding markets froze.

This point matters because financial crises are cumulative. A single weakness may be manageable, but a set of mutually reinforcing weaknesses can overwhelm ordinary safeguards. For that reason, the 2008 crisis is best understood as a chain of incentives and institutional gaps rather than as a single accident.

Repo, Collateral, and Maturity Mismatch

Repurchase agreements, or repos, allowed institutions to finance securities by pledging them as collateral for short-term borrowing. This funding was cheap and flexible in normal times. But it created maturity mismatch: long-term or risky assets were financed by short-term liabilities that had to be renewed frequently.

If collateral values fell, lenders demanded higher haircuts or refused to roll over funding. This forced borrowers to sell assets, pushing prices down further. The process resembled a bank run, but instead of depositors lining up outside a bank, wholesale lenders withdrew from funding markets.

The crisis showed that runs can occur in sophisticated markets. Liquidity is not only a property of assets; it is also a property of collective confidence. Once confidence disappears, assets that were previously liquid can become difficult to sell except at distressed prices.

This point matters because financial crises are cumulative. A single weakness may be manageable, but a set of mutually reinforcing weaknesses can overwhelm ordinary safeguards. For that reason, the 2008 crisis is best understood as a chain of incentives and institutional gaps rather than as a single accident.

Interconnected Balance Sheets

Financial institutions were connected through derivatives, funding markets, credit lines, guarantees, securities holdings, and payment obligations. Interconnection allowed risk sharing, but it also created channels for contagion. The distress of one institution could reduce the market value of assets held by others or raise doubts about counterparties.

Because many institutions used similar risk models and held similar assets, diversification at the individual level did not necessarily create diversification at the system level. When everyone tries to sell similar assets in a crisis, markets become one-sided.

This is the essence of systemic risk: actions that seem rational for one institution can be destabilizing when many institutions do them simultaneously.

This point matters because financial crises are cumulative. A single weakness may be manageable, but a set of mutually reinforcing weaknesses can overwhelm ordinary safeguards. For that reason, the 2008 crisis is best understood as a chain of incentives and institutional gaps rather than as a single accident.

Chapter 4 - The Crisis Unfolds

Early Warning Signals

The first visible signs appeared before the dramatic events of 2008. Rising mortgage delinquencies, falling housing prices, and losses in mortgage-related funds signaled that the assumptions behind structured products were weakening. In 2007, stress appeared in asset-backed commercial paper markets and in institutions exposed to mortgage securities.

Warnings were often interpreted as contained problems. Many policymakers and market participants initially believed that subprime losses would be manageable because the direct mortgage exposure seemed limited relative to the size of the financial system.

This judgment underestimated leverage, opacity, and network effects. The issue was not only the size of subprime mortgages but the way they had been embedded into securities, funding structures, and institutional balance sheets.

This point matters because financial crises are cumulative. A single weakness may be manageable, but a set of mutually reinforcing weaknesses can overwhelm ordinary safeguards. For that reason, the 2008 crisis is best understood as a chain of incentives and institutional gaps rather than as a single accident.

Bear Stearns, Lehman Brothers, and AIG

In March 2008, the rescue of Bear Stearns signaled that authorities feared disorderly failure in a major securities firm. The event showed that investment banks, despite lacking ordinary deposit bases, had become systemically important because of their connections to short-term funding and derivatives markets.

The failure of Lehman Brothers in September 2008 intensified panic. It caused losses, uncertainty, and a sudden reassessment of counterparty risk across global markets. The event did not create all the underlying problems, but it triggered a decisive collapse in confidence.

AIG required rescue because its credit derivatives exposure created enormous obligations linked to mortgage-related securities. Its distress illustrated how insurance-like contracts could transmit risk far beyond mortgage lenders and investment banks.

This point matters because financial crises are cumulative. A single weakness may be manageable, but a set of mutually reinforcing weaknesses can overwhelm ordinary safeguards. For that reason, the 2008 crisis is best understood as a chain of incentives and institutional gaps rather than as a single accident.

From Financial Panic to Economic Contraction

After September 2008, the crisis moved quickly from financial markets into the real economy. Credit conditions tightened, firms postponed investment, households reduced spending, unemployment rose, and international trade contracted sharply.

Banks under stress cut lending not only because they lacked capital but also because uncertainty made them cautious. Firms dependent on credit lines or trade finance faced pressure. Consumers whose housing wealth had fallen reduced consumption.

The crisis therefore became a macroeconomic crisis. A financial shock reduced aggregate demand, and weak demand worsened credit quality, creating a feedback loop between banks and the real economy.

This point matters because financial crises are cumulative. A single weakness may be manageable, but a set of mutually reinforcing weaknesses can overwhelm ordinary safeguards. For that reason, the 2008 crisis is best understood as a chain of incentives and institutional gaps rather than as a single accident.

Chapter 5 - Policy Responses and Emergency Measures

Central Bank Liquidity

Central banks responded with emergency liquidity facilities, interest-rate cuts, currency swap lines, and support for stressed funding markets. The goal was to prevent liquidity shortages from becoming waves of insolvency and to keep payment and credit systems functioning.

Lender-of-last-resort policy is designed for moments when solvent institutions cannot obtain liquidity. In 2008, however, the distinction between liquidity and solvency was difficult. Falling asset prices made institutions look insolvent, while market panic made assets difficult to value.

The scale of central bank intervention expanded the traditional toolkit. Authorities had to support not only commercial banks but also money markets, primary dealers, asset-backed securities markets, and global dollar funding channels.

This point matters because financial crises are cumulative. A single weakness may be manageable, but a set of mutually reinforcing weaknesses can overwhelm ordinary safeguards. For that reason, the 2008 crisis is best understood as a chain of incentives and institutional gaps rather than as a single accident.

Bank Recapitalization and Guarantees

Governments injected capital into banks, guaranteed liabilities, raised deposit insurance limits, and in some cases nationalized or restructured institutions. These actions were controversial but aimed at stopping panic and restoring confidence.

Capital injections addressed a core problem: losses had eroded bank equity. A bank without adequate capital may survive day to day but will restrict lending and remain vulnerable to shocks. Recapitalization was therefore both a financial stability measure and a macroeconomic policy.

Guarantees created moral hazard concerns because they protected creditors and institutions from losses. Yet policymakers argued that in a systemic panic, allowing broad collapse could impose even greater costs on households, firms, and public finances.

This point matters because financial crises are cumulative. A single weakness may be manageable, but a set of mutually reinforcing weaknesses can overwhelm ordinary safeguards. For that reason, the 2008 crisis is best understood as a chain of incentives and institutional gaps rather than as a single accident.

Fiscal Stimulus and Demand Support

As output fell and unemployment rose, governments adopted fiscal stimulus packages. These included tax cuts, public spending, transfers to households, support for state and local governments, infrastructure programs, and automatic stabilizers such as unemployment benefits.

Fiscal policy was necessary because monetary policy alone could not restore demand once interest rates approached the lower bound and private balance sheets were impaired. Stimulus aimed to replace missing private spending with public demand.

The size, composition, and duration of stimulus became matters of debate. Some argued for aggressive spending to prevent depression; others worried about public debt. The post-crisis years showed that premature austerity can slow recovery when private demand remains weak.

This point matters because financial crises are cumulative. A single weakness may be manageable, but a set of mutually reinforcing weaknesses can overwhelm ordinary safeguards. For that reason, the 2008 crisis is best understood as a chain of incentives and institutional gaps rather than as a single accident.

Chapter 6 - Global Transmission

Why a U.S. Mortgage Crisis Became Global

The crisis began in U.S. mortgage markets but became global because financial institutions around the world held dollar assets, depended on dollar funding, or were connected to U.S. banks through derivatives and money markets.

European banks were significant purchasers of U.S. structured products and were also active in dollar funding markets. When dollar liquidity tightened, the Federal Reserve established swap lines with other central banks to ease global funding pressures.

This revealed the centrality of the dollar-based financial system. Even institutions outside the United States could experience dollar shortages if their assets and liabilities were mismatched by currency and maturity.

This point matters because financial crises are cumulative. A single weakness may be manageable, but a set of mutually reinforcing weaknesses can overwhelm ordinary safeguards. For that reason, the 2008 crisis is best understood as a chain of incentives and institutional gaps rather than as a single accident.

Trade, Commodities, and Emerging Markets

The crisis spread through trade as demand in advanced economies collapsed. Export-oriented economies saw orders fall, shipping declined, and commodity prices became volatile. Countries less exposed to toxic assets still suffered through weaker external demand.

Emerging markets faced capital flow reversals, exchange-rate pressure, and tighter financing conditions. Some were more resilient because they had stronger reserves and less foreign-currency debt than in previous crises. Others faced severe contractions.

The transmission demonstrated that financial globalization and trade integration can carry shocks quickly. Even countries with prudent domestic banking systems can be affected when global credit and demand contract simultaneously.

This point matters because financial crises are cumulative. A single weakness may be manageable, but a set of mutually reinforcing weaknesses can overwhelm ordinary safeguards. For that reason, the 2008 crisis is best understood as a chain of incentives and institutional gaps rather than as a single accident.

Europe and the Sovereign Debt Link

In Europe, the financial crisis later interacted with sovereign debt problems. Bank rescues increased public liabilities, recessions reduced tax revenues, and investors began questioning the fiscal sustainability of some governments.

The euro area faced additional institutional challenges because monetary union existed without a full fiscal union or banking union. Countries could not devalue individually, and the relationship between banks and sovereigns created a negative feedback loop.

The European experience showed that crisis management depends not only on policy instruments but also on institutional architecture. A currency union needs mechanisms for bank resolution, fiscal support, and lender-of-last-resort credibility.

This point matters because financial crises are cumulative. A single weakness may be manageable, but a set of mutually reinforcing weaknesses can overwhelm ordinary safeguards. For that reason, the 2008 crisis is best understood as a chain of incentives and institutional gaps rather than as a single accident.

Chapter 7 - Social and Distributional Consequences

Households and Foreclosures

The crisis had severe household consequences. Millions lost homes, many more lost housing wealth, and communities with concentrated foreclosures experienced falling property values, vacant houses, and social stress. The burden was uneven across regions, income groups, and racial communities.

Foreclosure was not only a legal event. It disrupted families, schooling, credit histories, neighborhoods, and local government finances. The social cost exceeded the outstanding balance of individual mortgages.

The housing collapse also weakened household balance sheets. When families owe more than their homes are worth, they reduce consumption and become less mobile. This slows recovery because household spending is a major component of aggregate demand.

This point matters because financial crises are cumulative. A single weakness may be manageable, but a set of mutually reinforcing weaknesses can overwhelm ordinary safeguards. For that reason, the 2008 crisis is best understood as a chain of incentives and institutional gaps rather than as a single accident.

Unemployment and Long-Term Scarring

Unemployment rose sharply during the recession. Job loss produced immediate income hardship and long-term scarring through skill depreciation, lower future earnings, and reduced labor force attachment. Young workers entering the labor market during the downturn faced particularly difficult conditions.

Long-term unemployment is costly because it can change both worker prospects and employer perceptions. Even after output begins to recover, labor markets may heal slowly if firms remain cautious and workers struggle to re-enter stable employment.

The crisis therefore affected human capital as well as financial capital. Economic crises are not measured only by GDP losses; they are also measured by delayed careers, lost businesses, mental stress, and weakened community institutions.

This point matters because financial crises are cumulative. A single weakness may be manageable, but a set of mutually reinforcing weaknesses can overwhelm ordinary safeguards. For that reason, the 2008 crisis is best understood as a chain of incentives and institutional gaps rather than as a single accident.

Inequality and Trust

The distributional effects of the crisis contributed to declining trust in institutions. Many citizens saw banks rescued while households faced foreclosure and unemployment. This contrast intensified debates about fairness, accountability, and the legitimacy of economic policy.

Asset price recovery benefited households that retained financial assets, while many lower-income households had limited exposure to equities and were more affected by job loss and debt. Recovery was therefore uneven.

The political consequences of the crisis included skepticism toward elites, anger at bailouts, and renewed debate about globalization, financial regulation, and the social contract. Financial crises can reshape political institutions as well as markets.

This point matters because financial crises are cumulative. A single weakness may be manageable, but a set of mutually reinforcing weaknesses can overwhelm ordinary safeguards. For that reason, the 2008 crisis is best understood as a chain of incentives and institutional gaps rather than as a single accident.

Chapter 8 - Reform and Regulation After 2008

Capital, Liquidity, and Stress Testing

Post-crisis reforms increased bank capital requirements, introduced liquidity standards, and expanded supervisory stress testing. The goal was to make banks better able to absorb losses and less dependent on unstable short-term funding.

Capital is the buffer that protects creditors and the public from losses. Liquidity regulation addresses the danger that a bank may have assets but not enough cash or marketable securities to meet withdrawals or funding needs.

Stress testing changed supervision by asking whether institutions could survive severe but plausible scenarios. It forced banks and regulators to think about correlated shocks rather than only average conditions.

This point matters because financial crises are cumulative. A single weakness may be manageable, but a set of mutually reinforcing weaknesses can overwhelm ordinary safeguards. For that reason, the 2008 crisis is best understood as a chain of incentives and institutional gaps rather than as a single accident.

Macroprudential Regulation

Macroprudential regulation focuses on the stability of the financial system as a whole rather than the safety of individual institutions in isolation. This approach emerged because the crisis showed that individually prudent behavior can become collectively dangerous.

Macroprudential tools include countercyclical capital buffers, loan-to-value limits, debt-to-income restrictions, systemic risk surcharges, and monitoring of nonbank credit intermediation. These tools aim to lean against credit booms before they become crises.

The challenge is political and technical. It is difficult to restrict credit during a boom because many participants benefit from rising prices. Yet prevention is most valuable precisely when it is least popular.

This point matters because financial crises are cumulative. A single weakness may be manageable, but a set of mutually reinforcing weaknesses can overwhelm ordinary safeguards. For that reason, the 2008 crisis is best understood as a chain of incentives and institutional gaps rather than as a single accident.

Resolution and Too Big to Fail

The crisis made clear that some institutions were considered too big, too complex, or too interconnected to fail in a disorderly way. This created moral hazard because creditors may expect protection and institutions may take greater risks.

Resolution reforms aimed to create procedures for winding down large financial institutions without destabilizing the entire system. Living wills, bail-in mechanisms, and special resolution authorities were designed to impose losses while preserving critical functions.

Whether too big to fail has been fully solved remains debated. The post-crisis system is more robust in many respects, but financial innovation and nonbank intermediation continue to create new forms of systemic importance.

This point matters because financial crises are cumulative. A single weakness may be manageable, but a set of mutually reinforcing weaknesses can overwhelm ordinary safeguards. For that reason, the 2008 crisis is best understood as a chain of incentives and institutional gaps rather than as a single accident.

Chapter 9 - Competing Interpretations

Market Failure and Incentives

One interpretation emphasizes market failure. Incentives rewarded short-term volume, fees, and leverage while underweighting long-term credit quality. Information asymmetry made it difficult for final investors to evaluate underlying loans, and conflicts of interest distorted ratings and underwriting.

From this perspective, the crisis demonstrates that financial markets require rules because private contracts do not automatically internalize systemic externalities. A lender may profit from a risky loan while society bears the cost of widespread defaults and unemployment.

The policy implication is stronger supervision, better incentives, transparent securitization, and tools that limit leverage during booms.

This point matters because financial crises are cumulative. A single weakness may be manageable, but a set of mutually reinforcing weaknesses can overwhelm ordinary safeguards. For that reason, the 2008 crisis is best understood as a chain of incentives and institutional gaps rather than as a single accident.

Policy Error and Monetary Conditions

Another interpretation emphasizes policy error. Critics argue that low interest rates, housing policies, government-sponsored enterprises, and regulatory gaps encouraged excessive mortgage credit. They argue that public policy helped create the conditions for the boom.

This view highlights how monetary policy and political incentives can shape risk-taking. When interest rates are low for extended periods, investors may reach for yield and households may take on larger debts.

The strongest explanations do not need to choose only between market failure and policy error. The crisis involved an interaction between public rules, private incentives, global capital flows, institutional design, and cognitive biases.

This point matters because financial crises are cumulative. A single weakness may be manageable, but a set of mutually reinforcing weaknesses can overwhelm ordinary safeguards. For that reason, the 2008 crisis is best understood as a chain of incentives and institutional gaps rather than as a single accident.

Minsky and Financial Instability

Hyman Minsky's financial instability hypothesis became prominent after the crisis because it explains how stability can produce risk-taking. As memories of crisis fade, borrowers and lenders move from hedge finance toward speculative and Ponzi finance, making the system vulnerable to reversal.

The Minsky framework emphasizes balance sheets, leverage, and cash-flow commitments. It is particularly useful for understanding why a small decline in asset prices can become a major crisis when many actors depend on rising prices and easy refinancing.

The crisis does not prove that markets are always unstable, but it supports the idea that capitalist financial systems require countercyclical safeguards because private optimism can become self-reinforcing.

This point matters because financial crises are cumulative. A single weakness may be manageable, but a set of mutually reinforcing weaknesses can overwhelm ordinary safeguards. For that reason, the 2008 crisis is best understood as a chain of incentives and institutional gaps rather than as a single accident.

Chapter 10 - Lessons for the Future

Lesson One: Watch the System, Not Only the Firm

The first lesson is that supervision must look beyond individual institutions. A bank may appear safe while the system becomes fragile because many institutions hold similar assets, depend on similar funding, or use similar models.

System-wide indicators include credit growth, leverage, asset prices, underwriting standards, maturity mismatch, and concentration in funding markets. These indicators are not perfect forecasts, but they can reveal vulnerability before crisis strikes.

Financial stability policy therefore requires humility. Regulators cannot predict every shock, but they can reduce the probability that ordinary shocks become catastrophic.

This point matters because financial crises are cumulative. A single weakness may be manageable, but a set of mutually reinforcing weaknesses can overwhelm ordinary safeguards. For that reason, the 2008 crisis is best understood as a chain of incentives and institutional gaps rather than as a single accident.

Lesson Two: Complexity Is Not the Same as Safety

Financial innovation can improve allocation of capital, but complexity can obscure risk. If an instrument is understood only through a model, and the model depends on optimistic assumptions, the appearance of precision may be misleading.

Complexity also affects accountability. When risks are sliced, sold, insured, and reassembled, it becomes difficult to identify who ultimately bears the loss. In a crisis, that uncertainty freezes markets.

The lesson is not to reject innovation but to demand transparency, adequate capital, robust stress scenarios, and simpler structures where possible.

This point matters because financial crises are cumulative. A single weakness may be manageable, but a set of mutually reinforcing weaknesses can overwhelm ordinary safeguards. For that reason, the 2008 crisis is best understood as a chain of incentives and institutional gaps rather than as a single accident.

Lesson Three: Crisis Response Must Protect the Economy, Not Only Finance

Emergency support for financial institutions may be necessary, but legitimacy depends on whether policy also protects households, employment, and productive capacity. If rescues are perceived as protecting only creditors and executives, public trust erodes.

A balanced response includes financial stabilization, demand support, foreclosure mitigation, unemployment assistance, and measures that preserve small business credit. The real economy must be at the center of crisis management.

The 2008 crisis taught that financial repair and social repair are connected. A stable banking system is essential, but stability without broad recovery remains politically and economically incomplete.

This point matters because financial crises are cumulative. A single weakness may be manageable, but a set of mutually reinforcing weaknesses can overwhelm ordinary safeguards. For that reason, the 2008 crisis is best understood as a chain of incentives and institutional gaps rather than as a single accident.

Timeline of Key Events

Date	Event	Significance
2001-2004	Low interest rates and rapid credit growth	Mortgage borrowing expands and risk premiums compress.
2004-2006	Housing prices and subprime lending surge	Underwriting standards weaken and securitization volumes rise.
2006	U.S. housing prices begin to turn	Refinancing becomes harder for vulnerable borrowers.
2007	Mortgage losses spread to structured products	Asset-backed commercial paper and funding markets show stress.
March 2008	Bear Stearns rescue	Authorities recognize systemic risk in investment banking.
September 2008	Lehman Brothers bankruptcy	Global panic intensifies and counterparty risk rises sharply.
September 2008	AIG rescue	Derivative exposure and interconnectedness become central policy concerns.
October 2008	Bank recapitalization and guarantees	Governments intervene to stabilize banks and funding markets.
2009	Stress tests and fiscal stimulus	Authorities attempt to restore confidence and support demand.
2010 onward	Regulatory reforms	Capital, liquidity, resolution, and macroprudential frameworks are strengthened.

The timeline shows that the crisis did not begin with one event. It developed as housing-market weakness exposed financial structures that had become dependent on continued confidence. By the time Lehman failed, the system was already fragile.

Timelines are useful because they prevent retrospective simplification. The crisis unfolded over years, with warnings, partial responses, and shifting interpretations. It is therefore important to distinguish early vulnerability, acute panic, and prolonged recovery.

Core Concepts

Leverage

The use of borrowed funds to increase exposure to assets. Leverage raises returns in good times but magnifies losses when asset values fall.

In the 2008 crisis this concept became practical rather than theoretical. Policymakers had to decide, often under extreme time pressure, how the concept applied to institutions, markets, and households.

Liquidity

The ability to meet cash obligations or sell assets without large price discounts. Market liquidity can disappear during panic.

In the 2008 crisis this concept became practical rather than theoretical. Policymakers had to decide, often under extreme time pressure, how the concept applied to institutions, markets, and households.

Solvency

The condition in which assets exceed liabilities. A solvent institution can still fail if it cannot obtain liquidity.

In the 2008 crisis this concept became practical rather than theoretical. Policymakers had to decide, often under extreme time pressure, how the concept applied to institutions, markets, and households.

Securitization

The process of pooling loans and transforming their cash flows into marketable securities.

In the 2008 crisis this concept became practical rather than theoretical. Policymakers had to decide, often under extreme time pressure, how the concept applied to institutions, markets, and households.

Maturity mismatch

Financing long-term assets with short-term liabilities, creating rollover risk.

In the 2008 crisis this concept became practical rather than theoretical. Policymakers had to decide, often under extreme time pressure, how the concept applied to institutions, markets, and households.

Systemic risk

The risk that distress in one part of the financial system disrupts the functioning of the wider economy.

In the 2008 crisis this concept became practical rather than theoretical. Policymakers had to decide, often under extreme time pressure, how the concept applied to institutions, markets, and households.

Moral hazard

A situation in which protection from losses encourages greater risk-taking.

In the 2008 crisis this concept became practical rather than theoretical. Policymakers had to decide, often under extreme time pressure, how the concept applied to institutions, markets, and households.

Macroprudential policy

Regulation aimed at the stability of the financial system as a whole.

In the 2008 crisis this concept became practical rather than theoretical. Policymakers had to decide, often under extreme time pressure, how the concept applied to institutions, markets, and households.

Case Study: Lehman Brothers

Lehman Brothers became the symbol of the crisis because its bankruptcy was followed by a severe collapse in confidence. The firm was deeply connected to funding markets, derivatives, prime brokerage, and global counterparties. Its failure raised uncertainty about exposures across the system.

The policy decision not to rescue Lehman remains debated. Some argue that the authorities lacked legal tools or sufficient collateral to support the firm. Others argue that the failure intensified panic and that a different resolution could have reduced systemic damage.

The lesson is that large financial institutions require credible resolution mechanisms before a crisis. Improvisation during panic is costly because uncertainty itself becomes a source of contagion.

Lehman also illustrates the danger of relying on short-term wholesale funding. When counterparties lose confidence, access to funding can disappear faster than assets can be sold at fair value. This liquidity pressure can destroy firms that appear viable in normal markets.

Case Study: AIG

AIG was not a conventional mortgage lender, yet it became central to the crisis through credit default swaps and guarantees linked to structured financial products. Its distress showed that systemic risk can accumulate outside ordinary banking channels.

The rescue of AIG was controversial because it protected counterparties and involved enormous public support. Policymakers feared that failure would create losses and uncertainty throughout the global financial system.

The case demonstrates how insurance-like contracts can create financial leverage. If guarantees are written without sufficient collateral and capital, the guarantor may become a point of systemic failure.

AIG also influenced post-crisis debate about derivatives clearing, collateral requirements, and the supervision of systemically important nonbank financial institutions.

Case Study: Households and Mortgage Debt

The household side of the crisis is sometimes overshadowed by bank failures, but mortgage debt was central to the origin and social cost of the crisis. Families took on obligations that depended on stable employment, refinancing access, and rising or stable house prices.

When house prices fell, many homeowners entered negative equity. This weakened consumption, reduced mobility, and increased default risk. A household balance-sheet recession can persist even after financial markets stabilize.

Policy responses to household distress were uneven and often slower than support for financial institutions. This difference contributed to public anger and to a perception that crisis management favored Wall Street over ordinary borrowers.

The household case shows why consumer protection and macroprudential policy are connected. Lending standards are not only private contract terms; at scale, they influence financial stability.

Discussion Questions

- Was the 2008 crisis primarily a failure of markets, regulation, monetary policy, or governance? Explain how these causes interacted.
- Why did securitization spread risk in theory but concentrate risk in practice?
- Should governments rescue financial institutions in systemic crises? Under what conditions?
- How can policymakers reduce moral hazard while preventing economic collapse?
- What indicators should regulators monitor during a credit boom?
- Why is household debt important for macroeconomic recovery?
- Can a future crisis be prevented, or only made less damaging?
- What are the advantages and limits of stress testing?
- How does financial globalization change the management of national crises?
- What social consequences should be included when evaluating crisis policy?

These questions are designed for classroom discussion, seminar writing, or independent reflection. They encourage readers to connect technical financial mechanisms with political and social consequences.

Extended Study Notes

The Role of Incentives

Incentives shape financial behavior more powerfully than official statements or ethical codes. Before the crisis, compensation systems often rewarded loan volume, securitization fees, trading profits, and short-term returns. Losses, however, could appear only years later. This timing mismatch encouraged decisions that appeared profitable in quarterly results but created hidden fragility.

Good crisis analysis therefore asks who was rewarded, when the reward appeared, and who ultimately bore the loss. Mortgage brokers were not the only actors with distorted incentives. Investors, rating agencies, managers, and public officials also faced incentives to accept optimistic assumptions during the boom.

Reforming incentives is difficult because risk-taking is profitable in expansions. A system that punishes only after collapse will always be late. Prevention requires rules that operate while the boom is still politically popular.

Why Liquidity Matters

Liquidity is often invisible until it disappears. Before 2008, many institutions believed that they could sell assets or borrow against them whenever needed. That belief allowed balance sheets to become larger and more dependent on continuous market functioning.

When doubts rose, liquidity vanished. Buyers demanded large discounts, lenders raised haircuts, and institutions that depended on rolling over short-term funding faced immediate pressure. What had looked like a stable funding model became a run-prone structure.

The crisis demonstrates that liquidity risk is not separate from solvency risk. If illiquidity forces asset sales at distressed prices, accounting losses can erode capital and create real insolvency.

The Psychology of the Boom

Booms are sustained not only by money but also by narratives. Before 2008, many believed that housing prices were unlikely to fall nationally, that financial engineering had dispersed risk, and that sophisticated institutions could manage complex exposures. These beliefs made caution appear old-fashioned.

Human psychology contributes to crisis through extrapolation, herding, overconfidence, and confirmation bias. Market participants often interpret rising prices as evidence that their assumptions are correct. Rising collateral values then permit more borrowing, which pushes prices higher still.

Because psychology is part of finance, regulation cannot rely only on disclosure. People may ignore warnings when profits are strong. Countercyclical rules are intended to restrain behavior when optimism is excessive.

The Function of Capital

Capital is sometimes described as idle money, but in banking it is a crucial form of resilience. It allows institutions to absorb losses without defaulting on creditors or cutting credit abruptly. Thin capital makes a financial system more profitable in good times and more dangerous in bad times.

The crisis revealed that some institutions had too little true loss-absorbing capacity relative to their risks. Off-balance-sheet vehicles, structured exposures, and risk-weighted models made vulnerability harder to see.

Post-crisis capital reform therefore aimed not only to increase the amount of capital but also to improve its quality and comparability. The lesson is simple: a financial system with weak equity buffers asks the public to become the final shock absorber.

Crisis Communication

Communication is itself a policy instrument during panic. Authorities must explain what they are doing, why they are doing it, and how support will be limited or conditioned. Poor communication can intensify uncertainty even when the policy action is substantively strong.

In 2008, policymakers faced the challenge of calming markets while acknowledging serious risks. If they sounded too optimistic, they lost credibility; if they sounded too alarmed, they risked accelerating panic.

The communication lesson is that credibility must be built before a crisis. Institutions trusted in normal times are more likely to be believed when they must act quickly under stress.

The Importance of Data

One difficulty in 2008 was that authorities and investors did not always know where risk was located. Complex securitization chains obscured exposures. Some institutions had direct mortgage exposure; others had guarantees, liquidity commitments, or derivative links.

A modern financial system requires timely data on leverage, funding, collateral, derivatives, and interconnectedness. Without such information, policymakers respond in fog. They may overreact in some areas and underreact in others.

Data alone does not prevent crises, but it improves diagnosis. A doctor cannot treat effectively without vital signs; a regulator cannot supervise a system whose risks are hidden in opaque markets.

Consumer Protection and Stability

Consumer protection is often treated as separate from financial stability, but the mortgage crisis showed that the two are connected. Widespread unaffordable lending can damage households and also undermine the securities, banks, and investors connected to those loans.

If loans are designed around borrower confusion or unrealistic refinancing assumptions, the problem is not merely individual unfairness. At scale, such loans become macrofinancial risk.

This is why post-crisis reform included attention to mortgage disclosure, ability-to-repay standards, and consumer financial supervision. Protecting borrowers can also protect the system.

Why Recovery Was Slow

Recovery after the crisis was slow because the shock damaged balance sheets. Households reduced debt, banks repaired capital, firms delayed investment, and governments debated the limits of fiscal support. This created a prolonged period of weak demand.

Balance-sheet recessions differ from ordinary inventory recessions. Lower interest rates may not generate rapid borrowing if households and firms are trying to reduce debt. Policy must therefore address debt overhang as well as the price of credit.

The slow recovery contributed to political dissatisfaction. Even when financial markets stabilized, many households experienced years of insecurity, weak wage growth, and damaged wealth.

The Role of International Coordination

Because the crisis crossed borders, national policies were not enough. Central bank swap lines, coordinated interest-rate cuts, international financial forums, and shared regulatory standards all became part of the response.

International coordination is difficult because countries face different domestic pressures. A policy that stabilizes global markets may be unpopular nationally if it appears to support foreign institutions.

Nevertheless, the crisis showed that financial sovereignty is limited in an interconnected system. No major economy can fully insulate itself from global funding shocks and synchronized demand contractions.

Moral Hazard Revisited

Moral hazard is a real concern. If investors expect rescue, they may lend too cheaply to risky institutions. If managers expect support, they may take excessive risks. Yet refusing support during systemic panic can destroy ordinary businesses and households that did not create the risk.

The policy challenge is to separate emergency stabilization from unconditional protection. A rescue can be paired with management removal, shareholder losses, restructuring, fees, regulation, and later resolution reform.

The best answer to moral hazard is not to promise never to intervene. It is to build a system where intervention protects essential functions while imposing losses on those who knowingly accepted risk.

The Shadow Banking Challenge Today

Post-crisis reforms strengthened banks, but risk can migrate. If regulated banks become safer, some credit activity may shift to nonbank financial institutions, private funds, fintech platforms, or market-based vehicles.

This migration does not necessarily mean danger, but it requires monitoring. The same maturity mismatch and leverage that weakened banks can appear in new institutional forms.

The enduring lesson is functional regulation: authorities should focus on what an activity does, not only on the legal label of the institution performing it.

Historical Memory

Financial history is a form of public infrastructure. When memories of crisis fade, pressure for strict standards weakens. Market participants may begin to view safeguards as unnecessary burdens rather than as protections purchased by hard experience.

Historical study helps counter this forgetting. The 2008 crisis should be taught not as a fixed story of villains and victims but as a system failure with recurring patterns visible in earlier crises.

Every generation tends to believe its financial innovations are safer than older forms of credit. History warns that innovation changes the form of risk more often than it abolishes risk.

Conclusion

The 2008 economic crisis was a defining event in modern economic history. It revealed the fragility of a financial system that had become highly leveraged, complex, interconnected, and dependent on confidence in asset prices and short-term funding.

The crisis began in mortgage markets but expanded because risk had been transformed and distributed through securities, derivatives, and funding channels. It became a global macroeconomic crisis because financial systems and real economies are inseparable.

The response prevented an even deeper collapse, but it also generated difficult questions about fairness, moral hazard, public debt, institutional legitimacy, and the distribution of recovery. These questions remain relevant because future crises will also require rapid choices under uncertainty.

The lasting lesson is not that finance is inherently destructive. Finance is essential for investment, innovation, housing, trade, and growth. The lesson is that finance must be governed by institutions capable of resisting boom-time complacency and crisis-time panic.

If the crisis teaches one principle above all, it is that stability must be built before it is needed. Capital, transparency, consumer protection, macroprudential tools, credible resolution regimes, and social safety nets are not luxuries. They are the infrastructure of resilience.

Glossary

Asset-backed security. A security backed by a pool of loans or receivables.

Bailout. Public or institutional support designed to prevent failure or systemic disruption.

Collateralized debt obligation. A structured product backed by pools of debt instruments, often divided into tranches.

Credit default swap. A derivative contract that provides protection against default or credit events.

Deleveraging. The process of reducing debt or financial exposure.

Haircut. The discount applied to collateral value in secured lending.

Liquidity trap. A situation in which monetary policy becomes less effective because interest rates are near zero and demand remains weak.

Quantitative easing. Central bank purchases of assets to lower long-term rates and support financial conditions.

Subprime mortgage. A mortgage to a borrower with weaker credit characteristics.

Too big to fail. The perception that an institution is so important that authorities will prevent its disorderly failure.

References

Bank for International Settlements. (2009). 79th Annual Report. Basel: BIS.

Bernanke, B. S. (2015). The Courage to Act: A Memoir of a Crisis and Its Aftermath. New York: W. W. Norton.

Blanchard, O. (2009). The crisis: Basic mechanisms and appropriate policies. IMF Working Paper.

Brunnermeier, M. K. (2009). Deciphering the liquidity and credit crunch 2007-2008. Journal of Economic Perspectives, 23(1), 77-100.

Financial Crisis Inquiry Commission. (2011). The Financial Crisis Inquiry Report. Washington, DC: U.S. Government Printing Office.

Gorton, G. B. (2010). Slapped by the Invisible Hand: The Panic of 2007. Oxford: Oxford University Press.

International Monetary Fund. (2009). World Economic Outlook: Crisis and Recovery. Washington, DC: IMF.

Kindleberger, C. P., & Aliber, R. Z. (2011). Manias, Panics, and Crashes: A History of Financial Crises (6th ed.). Basingstoke: Palgrave Macmillan.

Krugman, P. (2009). The Return of Depression Economics and the Crisis of 2008. New York: W. W. Norton.

Minsky, H. P. (1986). Stabilizing an Unstable Economy. New Haven: Yale University Press.

Rajan, R. G. (2010). Fault Lines: How Hidden Fractures Still Threaten the World Economy. Princeton: Princeton University Press.

Reinhart, C. M., & Rogoff, K. S. (2009). This Time Is Different: Eight Centuries of Financial Folly. Princeton: Princeton University Press.

Shiller, R. J. (2008). The Subprime Solution: How Today's Global Financial Crisis Happened, and What to Do about It. Princeton: Princeton University Press.

Taylor, J. B. (2009). Getting Off Track: How Government Actions and Interventions Caused, Prolonged, and Worsened the Financial Crisis. Stanford: Hoover Institution Press.

Tooze, A. (2018). Crashed: How a Decade of Financial Crises Changed the World. New York: Viking.

United States Department of the Treasury. (2009). Financial Regulatory Reform: A New Foundation. Washington, DC.

World Bank. (2009). Global Development Finance: Charting a Global Recovery. Washington, DC: World Bank.

The references above are provided to guide further study. The book intentionally summarizes major debates rather than reproducing any single author's interpretation.

Publisher: Eliva Press Global Ltd

Email: info@elivapress.com

www.ingramcontent.com/pod-product-compliance
Lightning Source LLC
LaVergne TN
LVHW022321200926
848481LV00004B/1391
* 9 7 8 9 9 9 3 4 4 7 2 2 *